ONE GOOD TURN

by Una McKevitt

SAMUEL FRENCH

Copyright © 2021 by Una McKevitt
All Rights Reserved

ONE GOOD TURN is fully protected under the copyright laws of the British Commonwealth, including Canada, the United States of America, and all other countries of the Copyright Union. All rights, including professional and amateur stage productions, recitation, lecturing, public reading, motion picture, radio broadcasting, television, online/digital production, and the rights of translation into foreign languages are strictly reserved.

ISBN 978-0-573-13270-4

concordtheatricals.co.uk
concordtheatricals.com
Design by zoodigital.ie

FOR AMATEUR PRODUCTION ENQUIRIES

UNITED KINGDOM AND WORLD
EXCLUDING NORTH AMERICA
licensing@concordtheatricals.co.uk
020-7054-7200

Each title is subject to availability from Concord Theatricals, depending upon country of performance.

CAUTION: Professional and amateur producers are hereby warned that *ONE GOOD TURN* is subject to a licensing fee. The purchase, renting, lending or use of this book does not constitute a license to perform this title(s), which license must be obtained from the appropriate agent prior to any performance. Performance of this title(s) without a license is a violation of copyright law and may subject the producer and/or presenter of such performances to penalties. Both amateurs and professionals considering a production are strongly advised to apply to the appropriate agent before starting rehearsals, advertising, or booking a theatre. A licensing fee must be paid whether the title is presented for charity or gain and whether or not admission is charged.

This work is published by Samuel French, an imprint of Concord Theatricals. Ltd

The Professional Rights in this play are controlled by Concord Theatricals, Aldwych House, 71-91 Aldwych, London, WC2B 4HN.

No one shall make any changes in this title for the purpose of production. No part of this book may be reproduced, stored in a retrieval system, scanned, uploaded, or transmitted in any form, by any means, now known or yet to be invented, including mechanical, electronic, digital, photocopying, recording, videotaping, or otherwise, without the prior written permission of the publisher. No one shall share this title, or part of this title, to any social media or file hosting websites.

The moral right of Una McKevitt to be identified as author of this work has been asserted in accordance with Section 77 of the Copyright, Designs and Patents Act 1988.

USE OF COPYRIGHTED MUSIC

A licence issued by Concord Theatricals to perform this play does not include permission to use the incidental music specified in this publication. In the United Kingdom: Where the place of performance is already licensed by the PERFORMING RIGHT SOCIETY (PRS) a return of the music used must be made to them. If the place of performance is not so licensed then application should be made to PRS for Music (www.prsformusic.com). A separate and additional licence from PHONOGRAPHIC PERFORMANCE LTD (www. ppluk.com) may be needed whenever commercial recordings are used. Outside the United Kingdom: Please contact the appropriate music licensing authority in your territory for the rights to any incidental music.

USE OF COPYRIGHTED THIRD-PARTY MATERIALS

Licensees are solely responsible for obtaining formal written permission from copyright owners to use copyrighted third-party materials (e.g., artworks, logos) in the performance of this play and are strongly cautioned to do so. If no such permission is obtained by the licensee, then the licensee must use only original materials that the licensee owns and controls. Licensees are solely responsible and liable for clearances of all third-party copyrighted materials, and shall indemnify the copyright owners of the play(s) and their licensing agent, Concord Theatricals Ltd., against any costs, expenses, losses and liabilities arising from the use of such copyrighted third-party materials by licensees.

IMPORTANT BILLING AND CREDIT REQUIREMENTS

If you have obtained performance rights to this title, please refer to your licensing agreement for important billing and credit requirements.

ONE GOOD TURN was first produced by the Abbey Theatre, Ireland on 21st June 2021 for a limited in-person audience. It was also available to live stream and watch on-demand. Directed by Emma Jordan, Set Designer Colin Richmond, Costume Designer Enda Kenny, Lighting Designer Sarah-Jane Shiels, Sound Designer Carl Kennedy, Voice Director Andrea Ainsworth. The cast was as follows:

BRENDA	Catherine Byrne
FRANK	Bosco Hogan
FIONA	Liz FitzGibbon
AOIFE	Aoibhéann McCann
CIARAN	Shane O'Reilly
HELEN	Pom Boyd

Abbey Theatre | Amharclann na Mainistreach

Located right in the heart of Dublin, the Abbey Theatre is Ireland's National Theatre. It was founded by W.B. Yeats and Lady Augusta Gregory. Since it first opened its doors in 1904 the theatre has played a vital role in the artistic, social and cultural life of Ireland.

It may be steeped in history but its year round programme is a great mix of modern and classic plays from both Irish and international artists. There is also a wide variety of art forms, and on a given night you might also find dance, opera, music, and literary performances on either of its two stages.

Tickets start at €13 and are available on www.abbeytheatre.ie

Inspired by the revolutionary ideals of its founders and its rich canon of Irish dramatic writing, the Abbey Theatre's mission is to imaginatively engage with all of Irish society through the production of ambitious, courageous and new theatre in all its forms. The Abbey Theatre commits to lead in the telling of the whole Irish story, in English and in Irish, and affirms that it is a theatre for the entire island of Ireland and for all its people. In every endeavour, the Abbey Theatre promotes inclusiveness, diversity and equality.

The Abbey Theatre gratefully acknowledges the support of the Arts Council.

CHARACTERS

BRENDA
FRANK
FIONA
AOIFE
CIARAN
HELEN

AUTHOR'S NOTE

A few years ago, I wrote down a conversation between myself and my Dad where he was asking me to fix the reception on the TV and I was trying and failing to do that. I couldn't see where that conversation could go, so I put it away and only came back to it when I started working on *One Good Turn* in Spring 2020.

I was trying to capture something of the dynamics of caring for someone and being cared for by someone in the family home, the two sides of the experience. It can be a complicated time in a family and not something that skates off in your memory never to be seen again; it makes an impression.

I wanted as much as I could to reflect that shared experience back to an audience in a warm but honest way. But I didn't know where to start. As I sat in the shed staring into space, that scene with the TV came back to me, so I dug it up and started there.

Please note the character of Frank is being looked after at home by his family. Frank's health is in steady decline due to old age and emphysema but there is no terminal diagnosis/countdown at play in this family's life. The future is inevitable but uncertain.

Special thanks to Dramaturg Louise Stephens for taking me on this journey. This play is dedicated to my parents Ann and Pat McKevitt and my Godmother CeCilia Dunne.

(The McKenna family home. Late morning. **BRENDA** *is in the kitchen preparing Frank's breakfast. Upstage right is a staircase as seen in American 1980's sitcoms. Upstage centre a long window looks onto a back garden or patio or covered alley for storing coal bunkers and bikes, suburban looking. Upstage left is the back door with a small utility room with a washing machine. Fridges, presses etc... are upstage somewhere design dependent but not busy or retro or interesting, they've been incorporated into the room as sleekly as possible. These people have lived here a long time and kept on top of things. There are no antiques.)*

(Characters can be seen walking past the back window as they enter and exit, it's connected to the road. Midstage centre right is a small island food prep space and presses beneath and stage left of it a kitchen table and chairs. Downstage right is a door leading to Fiona's bedroom and ensuite and downstage centre right are Frank's armchair and a couch).

(There is a door stage left that leads to the rest of the house, to the living room and front door etc...)

*(***BRENDA*** is wearing a man's dressing gown and slippers with a white nightie underneath. She has white hair and although sleepy has the gait of a much younger woman,* **BRENDA** *has not leaned into her age. This is reflected in her style throughout.)*

(Vivaldi's Spring or something cheerful and familiar like it is playing on the radio.*)

*(**BRENDA** is busy making scones. When she puts one batch in she takes another batch out.)*

RADIO PRESENTER. And there we had Vivaldi's Concerto Number 1 in E Major. Spring. Allegro. Now we revisit our Mozart series this morning with Requiem Mass in D Minor.

*(**BRENDA** changes the radio station. It's a vox pop segment on the streets of Dublin. The presenter is an Irish man in his fifties. **FIONA** enters at some point during this.)*

*(**BRENDA** scoops up egg shells to put in the bin, when she presses the foot pedal rubbish falls out. She's not surprised by this but it is annoying. She picks it all up and presses it back in. **BRENDA** ties a knot in the rubbish bag and exits with it through the back door.)*

VOX POP (VO). Well, that sounds very hard Martin. Very hard. I know many of our listeners will sympathise with you there.

(Beat.)

Can I ask you now about that tattoo on your arm. It's of a young man, is that right?

MAN ON STREET (VO). My brother.

VOX POP (VO). I see. And what's your brother's name can I ask?

---

* Licensees must use a version of Vivaldi's Concerto Number 1 in E Major. Spring. Allegro in the public domain.

MAN ON STREET (VO). His name was Phil.

VOX POP (VO). Phil. That's short for Philip, isn't it?

MAN ON STREET (VO). Yeah.

VOX POP (VO). If you don't mind me asking Martin, is Phil still with us?

MAN ON STREET (VO). No.

VOX POP (VO). No. I see.

>*(Beat.)*

And can I ask what happened to Phil?

>*(**FIONA** puts one arm on the fridge and leans her head against it for emotional support.)*

FIONA. Ugh.

MAN ON STREET (VO). He died.

>*(**FIONA** takes a carton of milk from the fridge.)*

VOX POP (VO). I'm very sorry to hear that Martin. Very sorry for your loss.

>*(**FIONA** moves to the press to get a bowl and spoon.)*

And how, if you don't mind me asking, did he die?

FIONA. It's none of your business?

MAN ON STREET (VO). Four years ago, he died four years ago.

>*(**FIONA** makes her way to the table with her stash.)*

VOX POP (VO). And if you don't mind me asking, can I ask you now, was it a terribly tragic death?

FIONA. Jesus Christ Almighty.

> (**FIONA** *walks over and hits the radio off and moves back to the kitchen table.* **BRENDA** *re-enters. She notices the radio is off and turns around to turn it back on.*)

VOX POP (VO). So Mary you make two hundred euro a night, most nights. That's quite a lot of money.

MARY (VO). Not really.

VOX POP (VO). *(Traffic noises.)* And this is where you work most nights? This street and –

MARY (VO). Yeah. Up and around.

VOX POP (VO). And if you don't mind me saying Mary, you're very pale and you've no teeth to speak of?

FIONA. *(Looking at the radio in disbelief.)* What the fuck?

> (**FIONA** *stands up with her bowl, she's had enough. The next lines from Mary play under the exchange with* **FIONA** *and* **BRENDA**. *It can cut out at any time.*)

VOX POP (VO). And you're out here in all weather Mary, that's very hard. Very hard. I wouldn't like that, I'd be very used to the comfort of a nice home myself. And if you don't mind me asking you now Mary, how did you end up in your current circumstances? I'd say there was a tragedy in the family Mary, is that it, would that be how you ended up on the streets?

FIONA. I'm going to my room.

BRENDA. All right, all right, I'll turn it off.

> (**BRENDA** *turns off the radio.*)

FIONA. *(Sitting down.)* Thank you.

> *(Beat.)*

BRENDA. You're just like your father, d'you know that?

FIONA. Yes.

BRENDA. I can't understand why neither of you can listen to the radio –

FIONA. It makes a terrible, terrible noise.

BRENDA. – but you can watch any old rubbish on the television.

(Beat.)

I'll be turning it back on for the news, I don't care what you say I'm listening to the news.

FIONA. Is he up?

BRENDA. Someone in this house needs to know what's going on in the world.

FIONA. Is he awake Mam?

BRENDA. *(Poking around for sugar.)* There should be plenty of sugar here somewhere.

FIONA. Mam?

BRENDA. He's watching Bonanza.

(Beat.)

Where on earth did I put the sugar?

FIONA. He's obsessed with that show.

BRENDA. He's not obsessed with anything.

(Beat.)

FIONA. How's his back?

BRENDA. Was he asking you for cigarettes?

FIONA. What?

BRENDA. He's asking me to buy him cigarettes.

FIONA. No.

(*Beat.*)

Okay. Yeah. He did but I didn't give him any.

BRENDA.	**FIONA.**
The doctor said he's not to smoke.	– he's not to smoke. I know. I won't.

(**BRENDA** *gets a white plastic bag and fits it into the bin.*)

BRENDA. His back is fine now by the way.

FIONA.	**BRENDA.** (*simultaneously*)
Thank God.	He knows you didn't do it on purpose.

FIONA. Of course I didn't do it on purpose.

BRENDA. Although why you pulled the plug out of his bed I'll never know.

FIONA. He was complaining about a noise, a whirring sound, he said it was driving him mental –

BRENDA. I told you never to touch those plugs beside his bed –

FIONA. – and he kept calling me up and down the stairs to complain about this whirring noise –

BRENDA. – not to touch anything. The motor at the end of his bed makes a noise, it's always made a whirring noise. It's a motor.

FIONA. I nearly threw my back out going up and down the stairs to him looking for this noise.

BRENDA. He doesn't hear the whirring noise when the television's on so it's best to leave it on till he falls asleep.

FIONA. Why would no one tell me there's a motor pumping air into his mattress?

(Beat.) (Sulky.)

How was I supposed to know that?

BRENDA. The plug is connected TO THE BED. What did you think you were plugging out? I mean who in their right mind –

FIONA. He must have been so uncomfortable.

BRENDA. The poor man.

FIONA. But why didn't he say anything? He was literally lying on metal bars?

BRENDA. It's hardly his fault. He didn't plug it out, did he?

FIONA. I just think... maybe if there was a manual or something you could leave for when you go out –

BRENDA. A manual?

FIONA. It's a good idea. There's so many things to remember. The pills, his food, his –

BRENDA. Ah. So now it's my fault I didn't write a manual saying please do not deflate your father's bed the minute you're left alone with him?

*(**FIONA**'s face suggests she still thinks the manual is a good idea. **BRENDA** notices something on the counter.)*

Sorry, hold on a minute now, what happened here?

*(**BRENDA** puts her fingers on the island and pulls them off in an exaggerated fashion.)*

What in God's name happened here?

*(To **FIONA**.)*

Can you see that?

FIONA. *(Not looking.)* What?

BRENDA. *(Presses her fingers down and back up.)* Look.

> *(And again.)*

Look.

> *(And again.)*

Look.

FIONA. *(Looking over amused.)* What am I supposed to be looking at? I can't see anything?

BRENDA. The counter. It's all sticky.

> *(**BRENDA** spots a pan and picks it up to examine.)*

What was in this pan? It's ruined.

FIONA. *(Dumping more cereal in her bowl.)* I don't know, ask Aoife, I was in bed when she got in.

> *(**AOIFE** appears on the stairs wrapped in a towel and holding a wash bag and a small towel.)*

AOIFE. Ask me what?

BRENDA. What was in this pan?

AOIFE. What pan?

> *(**BRENDA** brandishes pan.)*

Oh that pan? I made a baked alaska when I got in from the airport last night.

> *(**FIONA** smirks as **BRENDA** looks confused.)*

BRENDA. A what?

FIONA. It's an ice-cream cake they serve at weddings.

BRENDA. I know what it is.

> (*To* **AOIFE**.)

What on earth possessed you?

AOIFE. I was starving and there was nothing to eat.

BRENDA. What do you mean there was nothing to eat, the house is falling down with food.

> (**AOIFE** *and* **FIONA** *exchange a look.*)

Is that why I can't find any sugar?

AOIFE. You have to use sugar to make the meringue Mam, there's no other way.

FIONA. And what d'you need a frying pan for?

AOIFE. Fuck off, Fiona.

BRENDA. (*Putting pan in bin.*) Ruined.

AOIFE. Ah… Mam. I just got home. Can we talk about this later? Please?

> (**AOIFE** *makes her way downstairs.*)

BRENDA. I left out bread from the freezer to eat, good bread for my diet, why didn't you eat that?

AOIFE. I didn't see any bread, did I?

BRENDA. And where did you get the ice cream from?

FIONA. (*Getting up with her bowl.*) I'm just gonna go to my room –

BRENDA. (*Pointing at her but not looking.*) Sit down and eat your breakfast.

> (**FIONA** *sits down again reluctantly.*)

AOIFE. There was ice cream in the freezer.

FIONA. Oh. God. No.

(Looks around at **AOIFE** *with horror mixed with pity.)*

Aoife.

AOIFE. What?

*(***BRENDA** *races to freezer, opens and roots through.* **AOIFE** *moves towards the exit downstage right.)*

BRENDA. Did I or did I not tell you both never to touch my ice cream?

FIONA. *(Putting her hands up.)* I didn't touch anything. I didn't touch it!

*(***BRENDA** *takes the ice-cream carton out of the freezer.)*

BRENDA. *(To* **AOIFE.***)* And you put the empty carton back in the freezer?

(Beat.)

Have you no respect?

AOIFE. I'm going into the shower Mam. We can talk about it later.

BRENDA. And what's wrong with the shower upstairs?

AOIFE. Nothing comes out of it. It feels like someone is crying on you.

FIONA. It's shit.

(Beat.)

BRENDA. Go on then but don't be all day in there and leave some hot water for Paul.

(Beat.)

Where is Paul? Is he still in bed?

AOIFE. No. He's still in London –

BRENDA. What? What about the wedding?

AOIFE. I'm going on my own.

BRENDA. Why?

AOIFE. We broke up.

BRENDA. Oh.

(Beat.)

That's a pity.

*(**AOIFE** moves towards the exit to the shower again but then stops.)*

AOIFE. *(To **BRENDA**.)* Why don't you come to the wedding with me?

BRENDA. I'm not going to a wedding.

AOIFE. It's only a registry office job, we can skip that and go straight to the dinner?

BRENDA. I've been to enough weddings.

AOIFE. I really don't want to go on my own.

BRENDA. Ask your sister. She's nothing to do.

*(They look at **FIONA**.)*

FIONA. Oh yeah, I'll go.

AOIFE. *(Cautious.)* Will you?

FIONA. Have we met?

AOIFE. Come on Mam, please. I really don't want to go on my own. And it'll be good for you to get out for a few hours.

BRENDA. I went out for three hours last night and she *(Pointing at **FIONA**.)* let the air out of your father's bed.

FIONA. It was an accident!

BRENDA. *(To* **AOIFE**.*)* And *you* ate all of my ice cream.

>   *(Beat.)*

Why would you do that?

AOIFE. I don't know, I- *(confused)*, looks at Fiona for help.

BRENDA. Why?

AOIFE. – everything was closed in the airport when I got in and I'd no dinner.

>   *(**BRENDA** is genuinely upset.)*

I didn't realise it was this critical.

>   *(Beat.)*

I'll go down and get some as soon as I have my shower, okay?

>   *(**AOIFE** exits stage right. **BRENDA** stays still a moment then gets back to the breakfast, some of the air let out of her tyres. **FIONA** watches her a moment.)*

FIONA. She said she'll replace it Mam.

BRENDA. That's not the point.

>   *(Beat.)*

Give that porridge a stir and put some garlic in it for me.

FIONA. Garlic?

BRENDA. He wants garlic in his porridge.

FIONA. Will garlic powder do?

BRENDA. No, it will not.

*(**FIONA** gets up and hunts the garlic down. **BRENDA** puts the cup of tea on a tray with a small jug of milk. **FIONA** pours porridge into a small bowl and crushes some garlic on top.)*

FIONA. *(Mimicking **VOX POP** man.)* So, Brenda. This breakfast is for your husband Frank. Would that be right?

*(**BRENDA** roots through a press and takes down a plastic bottle.)*

BRENDA. *(Squinting at the bottle.)* He'll have to make do with golden syrup. What date is on that?

*(**BRENDA** picks up her glasses and turns the bottle around and around looking for a date. **BRENDA** gives up and squeezes the syrup into the mug of tea.)*

FIONA. And can I ask you now Brenda, what is the matter with Frank? Touch of emphysema, is that it?

*(**BRENDA** nudges **FIONA** out of the way and starts rooting around for salt.)*

Little inflammation on the lungs?

BRENDA. Take the salt. Take it up to him with these.

*(**BRENDA** puts the scones on the tray picks it up and whirls it into **FIONA**'s hands.)*

FIONA. He'll never eat all that.

BRENDA. Just bring it up to him before it gets cold.

*(**FIONA** heads up the stairs still pretty skeptical about the tray's contents.)*

I'm giving back that rent you gave us by the way. We don't want it. Wait till you get a job and give us money then. We don't need it.

FIONA. Mam, keep the money. I have money. I'm not skint.

BRENDA. We don't want it. Put it into your pension.

FIONA. I don't have a pension.

BRENDA. Well. Get one.

> *(During this exchange* **CIARAN** *appears in the back window travelling towards the back door and carrying two large oxygen cylinders and a cloth bag on his shoulder.)*

> *(His granny Roisin lives next door to the family and* **CIARAN** *spent a lot of time there growing up, he's a good family friend and went to school with Aoife. He regularly visits his granny Roisin to assist with her care.)*

Hello, Ciaran love.

> *(To* **FIONA** *without looking up.)*

Fiona. Pour Ciaran a cup of tea.

> *(***FIONA** *gestures at the tray to indicate her hands are full anyway.)*

CIARAN. No, no, no, no, no, no tea. Thanks Fiona.

BRENDA. Where did you get those?

CIARAN. The back gate.

BRENDA. Did they take the old cylinders I left out?

CIARAN. They must have, they weren't there.

> *(Beat.)*

Unless, of course, I just brought the empty ones back in?

BRENDA. Don't say that.

(**BRENDA** *gestures for him to put them down on the kitchen table.* **BRENDA** *examines them.*)

(Inspecting the cylinders.) No, you see here, that's the seal, the green bit, so these two are new.

(Beat.)

Were you in with your grandmother, how's she doing? I called in yesterday but she seemed a bit tired so I didn't stay long.

CIARAN. The lovely woman is in with her now washing her hair. She loves that.

(**CIARAN** *takes a bottle out of his bag.*)

I brought the wheat grass I was telling you about.

BRENDA. What's this?

(**BRENDA** *sits down at the table and takes the bottle.*)

CIARAN. It's good for the lungs.

BRENDA. *(Very touched.)* Ah, that's very kind. Frank will love that.

CIARAN. He's brilliant, isn't he? You can give him anything. Gran won't even taste it for me.

BRENDA. Well, there's nothing wrong with your granny's lungs.

CIARAN. No, that's true.

BRENDA. She's marvellous, in there on her own.

CIARAN. But she's not on her own is she? There's always someone in on top of her. So she says anyway.

BRENDA. Is her appetite back up?

(Getting up quickly.)

You'll have a scone?

> (**BRENDA** *is back at the stove.* **CIARAN** *sits down at the kitchen table.*)

CIARAN. She had a bit of breakfast but – she's tired of it, you know?

> (**BRENDA** *picks up the wheat grass and unscrews the cap.*)

BRENDA. Frank used to soak natural bacterias and all sorts in jars and drink them.

You'd come down in the morning and there'd be scum floating on top of the jar and he'd just knock it back.

CIARAN. I think she'd a bad night's sleep.

BRENDA. Wicked! But I suppose they must have done him some good-considering how weak his lungs are –

CIARAN. A dark night for the should she calls it.

BRENDA. – they say he has the blood pressure of a young athlete.

CIARAN. She's afraid.

BRENDA. Golden syrup?

CIARAN. Oh my God. I remember eating scones here every day after school with Aoife. I was fat as a fool, I looked like a bloody trifle! Keep them away from me.

> (**CIARAN** *puts up a hand to ward her off.* **BRENDA** *puts the plate down and absentmindedly eats the scone herself/or gives it to* **CIARAN**.)

How are things anyway?

BRENDA. I must get dressed.

> (*Beat.*)

Good. You should try that new Indian down the road when you get a chance. We'd to wait half an hour for a table last night, so book in advance. You like Indian food, don't you? Or is that Fiona?

CIARAN. Me. Love it.

BRENDA. Oh. I've a few books your granny might read somewhere. Murders. I'll drop them into her later.

CIARAN. Do. She'll want to show off her clean hair.

BRENDA. When Frank and I first moved here we thought she was a movie star.

CIARAN. And she thought you were drug dealers.

(They laugh.)

She still talks about Frank's long hair.

BRENDA. God, it was desperate. And then he stuck a boat out in the back garden. You know she complained about it to the neighbourhood committee.

CIARAN. She has notions does Roisin.

BRENDA. Oh she does. You remember The Wilsons up the road? With the white van?

CIARAN. The woman cannot relax around a white van.

BRENDA. That poor man trying to make a living and up she marches asking him not to park his van in his own driveway.

(They laugh.)

I don't know that I'd ever have that kind of confidence.

CIARAN. Would you want it though?

BRENDA. I'd be too worried people wouldn't like me.

CIARAN. They wouldn't like you. They'd tell you to fuck off like they told her. And they'd be right.

BRENDA. Still.

(*Beat.*)

CIARAN. Are you thinking of anyone in particular?

BRENDA. No. Not the neighbours or anything, they can do what they want.

(*Beat.*)

I just admire how your granny always speaks her mind, she's not afraid of anyone. Frank's the same.

(*The doorbell rings.*)

Who's that at this hour?

CIARAN. The egg man. Don't tell him I'm here.

BRENDA. (*Flustered.*) The egg man?

(*Shouting up the stairs.*)

Fiona!

(*To* **CIARAN.**) I usually get six for your granny, will I?

CIARAN. I did her shopping this morning. She's plenty of eggs. Free range eggs.

FIONA. (*From upstairs.*) What!

BRENDA. (*To* **CIARAN.**) These are free range.

(*To* **FIONA.**) Do you know where my purse is!

FIONA. What!

CIARAN. (*Over "my purse is".*) They are in their hoop.

BRENDA. My. Purse. Where. It. Is?

FIONA. I can't hear you!

CIARAN. It's on Frank's chair.

(**BRENDA** *retrieves her purse.*)

BRENDA. What was it doing there?

> (**BRENDA** *exits stage left.* **FIONA** *arrives downstairs with three dirty cups, leaves them on the island and sits back down at the table.*)

FIONA. He says go up to him, he's decent.

CIARAN. *(Checking to make sure* **BRENDA** *can't hear.)* He phoned me this morning, you know?

FIONA. For a cigarette, I know, I heard him.

CIARAN. Poor Frank. Would you not give him one teeny weeny fag? Like what harm?

FIONA. No!

CIARAN. But d'you not think it's a bit hard on him, he's been smoking since he was ten.

FIONA. He gave up ages ago.

CIARAN. Says who?

FIONA. Says Brenda.

CIARAN. Gave up my hole. He just can't get his hands on one.

> (**BRENDA** *returns with a dozen eggs.*)

BRENDA. There's dirt and feathers on these eggs Ciaran, they're very fresh.

CIARAN. He glues those feathers on.

BRENDA. He does not glue them on!

> (**BRENDA** *puts the eggs down, picks off the feathers and pours herself a cup of tea. She puts the three cups* **FIONA** *left on the counter into the dishwasher under the island.*)

> (**AOIFE** *enters stage right still in the towel but now with a small towel wrapped round*

her head. She makes slow progress to a chair and picks up a newspaper and Brenda's cup of tea off the island absentmindedly. **FIONA** *and* **CIARAN** *watch her as she sits down and raises it to her mouth.)*

*(***BRENDA** *stands up from the dishwasher to take her tea, realises it's missing and spots* **AOIFE** *with it.)*

(Annoyed.) Please put down my tea Aoife.

AOIFE. Oh. Sorry.

*(***AOIFE** *spots* **CIARAN** *and laughs at her own semi nakedness.)*

Oh, hi Ciaran, you going to the wedding?

CIARAN. God no. I told them I was having an operation.

(Beat.)

So if they ask you haven't seen me.

(Beat.)

Where's Paul?

AOIFE. London.

CIARAN. *(Confused.)* What? Is he not –

FIONA. They broke up.

CIARAN. Oh Aoife. You idiot.

(Beat.)

So who are you going to take to the wedding?

FIONA. She could go on her own.

CIARAN. To a wedding? Are you out of your mind?

AOIFE. I'm trying to get Brenda to come with me.

BRENDA. The house is upside down and there's no one here to look after Frank, it's too short notice.

FIONA. I'm here to mind him.

BRENDA. *(To* **CIARAN.***)* I've nothing to wear anyway so it doesn't matter.

FIONA. You've millions of clothes. Millions. Every wardrobe in the house is full of your clothes.

AOIFE. It's her house Fiona.

FIONA. Yeah. I know it's her house Aoife.

(To **BRENDA.***)*

Just go, you'll have a great time. I'll look after Dad for you.

AOIFE. Please Mam, I really don't want to go on my own.

CIARAN. Don't go then. Say you're visiting me in the hospital.

AOIFE. I want to go, I came all the way home for it!

FIONA. *(To* **BRENDA.***)* I'll bring him up everything he needs, he'll love that. He can stay in bed for the day.

BRENDA. He is not staying in bed. D'you know how bad that is for him? He has to come downstairs.

FIONA. Okay.

BRENDA. Every day.

FIONA. I'll bring him down then.

BRENDA. For a few hours. Or he'll lose all mobility.

FIONA. Okay, okay I get it. He has to come downstairs.

BRENDA. And do his exercises. And you'll have to monitor his oxygen and mind his nose doesn't get sore from the tubes and help him up and down the stairs and don't let him fall when he's going to the bathroom. Can you do all that?

FIONA. Probably... most of it... he hates doing his exercises.

BRENDA. I know but he has to do them.

CIARAN. I'd say you could do with a night out Brenda, couldn't you? I know I could.

(Holding a finger up to **AOIFE**.*)*

Not a wedding! Maybe a good funeral though.

*(***CIARAN**'s *phone rings, he picks it up and looks at it. It's* **FRANK**.*)*

Speak of the devil.

*(***CIARAN** *answers her phone.)*

Hello Frank. I'm here, I'm downstairs. I'm coming up to you now.

I've been summoned.

BRENDA. *(To* **CIARAN**.*)* You can take him up the paper there, he'll want the crossword.

CIARAN. *(To* **FRANK**.*)* We're bringing you up the paper.

AOIFE. *(Pen pausing mid air.)* Oh.

FIONA. Aoife! You know that's for him!

CIARAN. *(To* **FRANK**.*)* Aoife might have gotten to the crossword.

AOIFE. How did I know?

FIONA. Come on!

CIARAN. *(To* **FRANK**.*)* They're giving out to her now.

AOIFE. I didn't! I swear to God I didn't!

BRENDA. Ah Aoife.

AOIFE. Sorry. I'm jet lagged.

FIONA. From London? Would you cop on.

> (**BRENDA** *takes the paper.*)

CIARAN. *(To* **BRENDA.***)* He says the tank is empty.

BRENDA. There's plenty left in it.

CIARAN. *(To* **FRANK.***)* She says there's plenty left in it.

BRENDA. The doctor said to leave the gauge at two and a half.

CIARAN. He says it's empty.

BRENDA. Alright, alright, tell him we'll bring up the new cylinders.

CIARAN. *(To* **FRANK.***)* We're bringing up the new cylinders.

> (**CIARAN** *hangs up.*)

I'll take the oxygen Brenda, you take the paper.

> (**CIARAN** *picks up the cylinders and heads towards the stairs.* **FIONA** *hands* **BRENDA** *over the newspaper.*)

BRENDA. And I might have a look and see if I've anything to wear upstairs but I can tell you now I don't have anything clean I could wear to a wedding.

> *(To* **AOIFE.***)*

What are you wearing?

AOIFE. Well. I was going to see if you had anything I could borrow.

BRENDA. What's wrong with the outfit you brought?

AOIFE. I don't have an outfit with me.

BRENDA. D'you mean to tell me you came over from London for a wedding with nothing to wear?

AOIFE. I left my suitcase at the airport.

CIARAN. At the airport, did they lose it?

AOIFE. No, I just, I forgot to pick it up when I landed.

BRENDA. How in God's name?

AOIFE. Don't start Mam.

CIARAN. What? So you left the airport with no bag?

AOIFE. I had some take on luggage and my purse from the plane and I just forgot I had another bag. It could happen to anyone.

*(**CIARAN** and **FIONA** exchange a look.)*

BRENDA. So it's still in the airport? That's very suspicious.

AOIFE. It's all right Mam, I rang them and they have it, I'm picking it up tomorrow on the flight back.

(Beat.)

BRENDA. *(Moving towards the stairs.)* What time is this wedding anyway?

AOIFE. We don't have to be there until about two-ish.

*(**CIARAN** and **BRENDA** head up the stairs.)*

BRENDA. And what am I supposed to do with my hair?

CIARAN. I think at your age once you keep your hair you really don't have to do anything else but give it a good wash and show it off.

BRENDA. What a thing to say Ciaran.

(Up the stairs.)

Frank. You've a visitor.

*(**CIARAN** and **BRENDA** exit scene.)*

(**FIONA** *picks up the tea pot, putting it down finding it empty.* **AOIFE** *sips her tea elegantly, there's a somewhat awkward pause.*)

AOIFE. So it must be weird being home?

FIONA. No.

AOIFE. No?

FIONA. Not really.

AOIFE. Okay.

> *(Drinking tea.)*

What time is he getting up these days?

FIONA. About midday. Usually later.

AOIFE. That's good.

> *(Beat.)*

He seems in good form to me.

FIONA. Yeah.

AOIFE. Skinnier.

FIONA. He's not that bothered with food.

AOIFE. But he's dying for a cigarette.

> *(They catch each other's eyes.)*

FIONA. Poor Frank.

> *(Beat.)*

AOIFE. You know he told me not to tell you anything.

FIONA. What? Why?

AOIFE. That you report it all back to Brenda.

FIONA. He's just annoyed I won't give him a smoke.

(Pause.)

AOIFE. So. How are you doing?

FIONA. *(Exasperated.)* I'm fine Aoife.

AOIFE. What?

(Beat.)

I'd go crazy living at home, that's all.

(Beat.)

Not having my independence.

FIONA. Oh, they let me out.

AOIFE. I know myself. I couldn't cope with the anxiety of not working

FIONA.	**AOIFE.** *(simultaneously)*
I've had lots of jobs.	that would terrify me.

AOIFE. Oh, I know!

FIONA. I've been working my whole life.

AOIFE. Of course!

FIONA. Since I was fifteen, I've always had jobs.

AOIFE. I'm not saying anything about that. I'm just talking about me.

FIONA. Right. You like your job, it's different.

AOIFE. I like making money, yeah.

BRENDA. *(From upstairs.)* Fiona! Fiona!

FIONA. *(Frustrated.)* Uuuuuuggggggggghhhhhhhhh.

*(**FIONA** goes to the bottom of the stairs.)*

(Shouting up.)

Please don't shout down the stairs at me Brenda. I've asked you a million times. It's very triggering. I'll come up.

(FIONA starts climbing stairs.)

BRENDA. Fiona!!

FIONA. Hold on! I can't hear you.

(The house phone rings.)

BRENDA. Fiona! Are you deaf?

FIONA. Just a minute Mam! I have to answer the fucking phone!

(FIONA picks up the house phone which possibly could be classed as an antique.)

Hello?

(Listens.)

Hi Mam. I heard you. I did answer.

(Listening.)

I think he drank the last one yesterday. Where? Okay. I will. No. There's nothing wrong with my hearing. I'm not getting my ears checked Mam. Goodbye.

(FIONA hangs up and starts opening presses in a mood.)

There definitely aren't any left –

(FIONA pulls a small box down from a top shelf.)

Oh.

(FIONA brings it over to the island and pulls some small plastic bottles from it.)

AOIFE. What are they?

FIONA. A kind of elderly milkshake. He loves them.

AOIFE. *(Getting up.)* Let me taste.

FIONA. No, Aoife, don't, gross.

> *(**AOIFE** crosses over to the island.)*

AOIFE. Have you never tasted it?

FIONA. No. I prefer food you can chew.

AOIFE. *(Picking one up.)* Oh, look they come with a straw. Cute.

FIONA. Don't say that.

AOIFE. Why not?

FIONA. It's condescending to call old people cute.

AOIFE. I didn't call him cute, I called the straw cute.

> *(**AOIFE** pops the straw in and takes a sip.)*

Not bad, tastes like banana.

> *(**CIARAN** appears at the top of the stairs.)*

CIARAN. *(Stretching out his hand.)* Your mother says you're taking too long.

> *(**FIONA** takes the drink out of **AOIFE**'s hand and hands it over to **CIARAN** who marches back upstairs again.)*

AOIFE. Shit, what time is it, I better get ready.

> *(**AOIFE** gets tired thinking about getting ready and pops her elbows down on the island with her head resting on her hands. **FIONA** tidies the table.)*

FIONA. Pity about Paul.

AOIFE. Don't start Fiona.

FIONA. She loves Paul.

AOIFE. She does not love Paul.

FIONA. She does love Paul.

>   *(Beat.)*

He's very handy.

>   (**AOIFE** *makes a face.*)

He is!

AOIFE. He fixed the shed door! Big Deal.

FIONA. He talks to her about Frank, about his breathing. She listens to him.

AOIFE. 'Cause he's a nurse.

FIONA. Something we could really do with in this family.

AOIFE. Why don't you become one then?

That could be your new career path –

FIONA. What are you talking about?

AOIFE. If we need a nurse so bad why don't you become one. What d'you think?

FIONA. Do you really think I've the right personality to be a nurse Aoife? Do you?

AOIFE. They're crying out for nurses.

FIONA. Aoife. I'm not becoming a nurse.

AOIFE. And I'm not staying with Paul just to keep my mother happy.

FIONA. Why not? Lots of people do.

AOIFE. Just because you feel bad about moving home –

FIONA. I don't feel bad. They said I could stay here until I worked out what I want to do.

AOIFE. What else are they going to say? Don't give up your job and start from scratch because you're nearly fifty?

FIONA. Fifty? Would you cop on.

(Beat.)

What has she been saying?

AOIFE. Nothing.

(Beat.)

She doesn't like you in your room all day.

*(**FIONA** sighs.)*

FIONA. I need to spend some time on my own.

AOIFE. She takes it personally.

FIONA. I don't have that much to say. I just can't talk that much.

AOIFE. That's pathetic.

FIONA. About everything Aoife! The chairs, the tables, the news, the shops, the neighbours… I just can't talk that much. I'm not chatty!

AOIFE. Well, she is. And this is her house.

(Beat.)

FIONA. I'm going to have to hit you with something if you keep on about that.

(Beat, angrier.)

I know whose house it is. I'm here.

AOIFE. Only because you've given up a perfectly good career.

FIONA. Career? What exactly is it you think I do?

AOIFE. Finance, accounting?

FIONA. Wow. I wish I'd known you were so invested in my life.

AOIFE. Well I don't know, you work in an office, don't you?

FIONA. I'm a clerical officer in an insurance company.

AOIFE. Brilliant. What's wrong with that?

FIONA. Nothing, I just don't want to do it anymore.

AOIFE. But that's what you're saying to me about Paul. That I should hold onto him, even though –

FIONA. Even though he's too good for you?

(Beat. They catch each other's eyes.)

AOIFE. D'you know how annoying it is? Everyone likes the fucker.

FIONA. Frank'll be devastated too.

AOIFE. I know. He keeps asking me when we'll have a baby. Does he ask you that?

FIONA. No.

(Beat.)

I'm only here for a few months, it's not permanent.

AOIFE. But how do you know?

FIONA. Because I'm working it out.

AOIFE. How?

FIONA. By – I'm –

AOIFE. How?

FIONA. By thinking. I'm thinking it out.

AOIFE. Right.

FIONA. And Mam needs help.

AOIFE. Did she say that?

FIONA. Someone has to be here with him all the time. It's hard for her to even get to the shops.

AOIFE. That's over the top, he's up there watching TV, he's fine for a few hours on his own.

FIONA. She won't leave him on his own. At least if there's someone here she can get out.

AOIFE. I have a job in London, I live in London.

FIONA. London, London. So far way.

AOIFE. I come home all the time.

FIONA. You don't.

AOIFE. You're only here because you're broke and it suits you.

FIONA. And you're only here because you're going to a wedding! A wedding of all fucking things. Who even gets married anymore?

AOIFE. Caroline and Maeve.

FIONA. Caroline Murphy?

(**AOIFE** *nods.*)

Okay, I feel bad. Caroline's nice. I hope her and Maeve are very happy.

(**AOIFE** *catch each other's eyes, amused.*)

AOIFE. I was actually trying to think of a career that might suit you on the flight over.

FIONA. Oh you were, were you? This should be good.

AOIFE. I was thinking you might make a good poet.

FIONA. A poet? Right.

AOIFE. What d'ya think?

FIONA. I think it's a bit late now to try and make a living writing poems.

AOIFE. You used to write great poems when we were kids.

FIONA. You did.

AOIFE. *(Amused.)* Oh, yeah.

(Beat.)

Well, you'll find something else to do.

FIONA. I'm doing nothing for a while.

(Beat.)

AOIFE. D'you think –

FIONA. What?

AOIFE. D'you think you might –

FIONA. Do you think I might?

AOIFE. Do you think you might be depressed or something?

(Beat.)

FIONA. Is that what Brenda said?

AOIFE. No. No one said anything.

FIONA. Because I'm not.

AOIFE. Oh, well that's good.

FIONA. Hold on.

(Beat.)

Are you depressed?

AOIFE. No. I just thought I'd ask if you were.

(Beat.)

And I did come home the last time he was ill.

FIONA. No, you didn't, you just happened to be here when he got sick.

AOIFE. I looked after him.

FIONA. You hid behind his bedroom door and pretended to be a ghost.

(**AOIFE** *laughs.*)

AOIFE. How do you remember that?

FIONA. How do I remember it? It's hardly an everyday occurence is it?

AOIFE. How would I know?

FIONA. Are you serious? Do you be well, do you? What is going on in your head?

(**BRENDA** *appears down the stairs dressed for the wedding.*)

AOIFE. *(To* **BRENDA.***)* You look nice Mam!

FIONA. *(To* **BRENDA.***)* Oooh. Gorgeous.

BRENDA. I was wondering about this scarf, is it too much?

AOIFE. D'you need it?

(**AOIFE** *takes the scarf from* **BRENDA.***)*

It's nice though.

(**AOIFE** *tries it on in the mirror.*)

FIONA. I think the scarf's okay, at least you can take it off, are you sure about those shoes though?

BRENDA. Why, what's wrong with my shoes?

AOIFE. Nothing.

FIONA. They're a bit matchy.

AOIFE. I like your shoes Mam.

> (**AOIFE** *ties the scarf in her hair.*)

I really like this scarf.

> (**BRENDA** *moves over to the mirror and looks at herself appraisingly. She likes what she sees.*)

BRENDA. You two don't know a thing about fashion.

> (*Turning to* **AOIFE.**)

Your hair is soaking wet, you'll get pneumonia. Go on and get dressed.

> (**AOIFE** *goes to make her way upstairs, the scarf still in her hair.* **BRENDA** *empties the washing machine, probably sheets.*)

Oh and will you take up your father's pills to him for me, I need to get this laundry out on the line.

> (**AOIFE** *stops in her tracks at "Oh".*)

And make sure he has a glass of water, will you?

> (**BRENDA** *exits out the back door. She turns right this time, not towards the back gate but towards the garden.*)

AOIFE. (*To* **FIONA.**) Where does she keep the pills?

FIONA. On the windowsill in the "days of the week" box.

> (**AOIFE** *walks over to the windowsill and takes out the pills and pours a glass of water. The sink could be on the island with the hob.* **AOIFE** *starts climbing the stairs. Just before she reaches the top she absentmindedly pops the pills in her mouth and drinks a gulp*

of water. **FIONA**, *having stood up to travel towards her room looks on in horror.)*

What the fuck Aoife?

(**AOIFE** *realises what she's done and screams.* **BRENDA** *runs back in the back door.)*

BRENDA. What? What? What happened!

AOIFE. Oh my God. Oh my God! I swallowed Dad's pills. What are they for? What are they for?

BRENDA. You did what?

(**CIARAN** *appears on the stairs.)*

CIARAN. What's going on?

FIONA. She swallowed Frank's pills.

BRENDA. Jesus! Aoife! What is wrong with you?

FIONA. Okay. Calm down.

CIARAN. How did this happen?

AOIFE. I don't know. I just put them in my mouth.

BRENDA. How many did you take?

AOIFE. All of them.

BRENDA. All of them!

AOIFE. All of them! Oh my God, I'm going to die, what am I going to do!

BRENDA. This box on the windowsill? Are you sure it was this box?

AOIFE. Yes? What are they for? What are they for?

BRENDA. They're for everything!

AOIFE. OH MY GOD!

BRENDA. Why would you do something like this!

FIONA. Okay, stop freaking out everyone! I'll ring Paul.

AOIFE. No!

BRENDA. Quick, I'll drive you down to the hospital, come on, hurry.

AOIFE. I'm not dressed!

FIONA. *(On her phone.)* Hold on. Let me ring Paul first.

BRENDA. *(To* **AOIFE.***)* Go and put some clothes on, now!

    *(***AOIFE*** doesn't move watching* **FIONA** *on the phone.)*

FIONA. *(To Paul.)* Paul, hi sorry, it's Fiona. I'm grand. Here, Aoife just swallowed Dad's pills. I don't know why. Because she's Aoife. Does she need to go to the hospital?

    (To **AOIFE.***)*

Do you think you can puke them up?

AOIFE. What? No! My stomach's empty.

CIARAN. I'll stick my fingers down your throat.

AOIFE. *(Sobbing.)* Mam, I want to go to the hospital.

BRENDA. *(To* **FIONA.***)* What does Paul say?

FIONA. Hold on.

    (To Paul.)

Yeah.

Yeah.

Yeah.

Yeah.

Hmmm. Yeah. Okay –

    *(***AOIFE*** is staring at* **BRENDA** *still in full crisis mode.)*

(To **AOIFE**.*)*

Does Paul know you've broken up?

AOIFE. Yes.

FIONA. Are you sure?

AOIFE. Yes!

FIONA. Sorry, what was that? Okay will do. Thanks so much Paul, you're a lifesaver.

(**FIONA** *hangs up the phone.*)

AOIFE. Well? What did he say?

FIONA. He said your silk pillowcase has arrived.

AOIFE. Fiona!

FIONA. You're fine, they're mostly for balance and blood pressure. You just can't drink or drive.

CIARAN. There goes the weekend.

(**BRENDA** *doesn't react.*)

FIONA. You okay, Mam?

AOIFE. I'm really sorry. It was an accident.

(*Everyone watches* **BRENDA** *nervously.*)

BRENDA. Your father needs his pills.

CIARAN. I'll bring them up, where's the box?

(**AOIFE** *points in the direction of the box.*)

BRENDA. He'll want some water.

CIARAN. *(Opening the box.)* I'll just take Sunday's pills will I, seeing as Aoife has gobbled all of Saturdays?

FIONA. Aoife, will you get dressed.

(**AOIFE** *picks up the glass of water and follows* **CIARAN** *up the stairs.*)

BRENDA. I was doing something?

FIONA. The clothes, I'll hang them up.

(**FIONA** *exits out the back door leaving* **BRENDA** *on stage alone for 60/90 seconds.* **BRENDA** *looks vulnerable and worn out.*)

(*Eventually she moves herself over to the kitchen table and sits down.*)

(**CIARAN** *comes back down the stairs carrying Frank's breakfast tray.*)

CIARAN. Frank can't believe it. He says Aoife would take the eyes out of your head if you let her.

(*He notices* **BRENDA**'s *mood and starts clearing away the breakfast stuff into the dishwasher, washing the scone pan, wiping the island down…*)

(**FIONA** *enters from the back door and* **AOIFE** *comes downstairs in one of Brenda's dresses.*)

AOIFE. When did you get this Mam –

FIONA. Mam?

AOIFE. – it's nice.

FIONA. *(To* **AOIFE.***)* Sshhh. Aoife!

(**CIARAN** *and* **FIONA** *move round to* **BRENDA.**)

CIARAN. Brenda, love?

(**CIARAN** *and* **FIONA** *tentatively sit down beside her.*)

BRENDA. *(Shaking her head.)* Don't mind me. There's nothing wrong with me, I don't know what I'm doing. I've nothing to cry about.

FIONA. Ah, Mam.

> *(Looking at **AOIFE**.)*

This is your fault. Do something.

AOIFE. *(Helplessly to **FIONA**/unspoken.)* What?

> *(**AOIFE** comes down the stairs.)*

Will I make a sandwich?

> *(To **BRENDA**.)*

Would you like a sandwich?

CIARAN. I'll make tea.

> *(**CIARAN** gets up to put the kettle on puts and **AOIFE** sits down.)*

AOIFE. I'm sorry about the pills Mam. I feel fine, there's nothing to worry about. I'm grand. There's nothing wrong with me.

> *(**CIARAN** makes a skeptical face.)*

FIONA. Forget about the pills Aoife, she needs more help, that's it isn't it Mam?

> *(**BRENDA** shakes her head and tries to pull herself together. The kettle boils and **CIARAN** pours it out into the cup.)*

BRENDA. You two have your own lives to be getting on with. Don't mind me. I'm just feeling sorry for myself.

> *(Beat.)*

I just feel, sometimes...

(She's trying to find the right words.)

he's so good and patient. I just feel like I'm horrible –

FIONA. To who? To Dad? No you're not.

AOIFE. Now come on, you do everything for him Brenda.

CIARAN. Do I leave the teabag in?

(AOIFE nods.)

FIONA. You're doing a great job Mam. You can't do everything. He's very demanding.

BRENDA. He is not, he asks for nothing.

FIONA. He's constantly asking for things!

BRENDA. *(Annoyed.)* Agh. You don't understand what I'm saying.

(CIARAN puts the tea in front of BRENDA and sits down.)

CIARAN. You can't be in top form all the time Brenda; it's mentally, physically and spiritually impossible.

BRENDA. I just feel like I'm always at him

FIONA. You're trying to keep him alive, that's all.

BRENDA. – getting him to do this and do that and he's tired –

FIONA	**BRENDA**
You just need a break Mam.	– and he doesn't want to do them.
A bit of help.	

BRENDA. *(Beat.)* I have help.

AOIFE. That lovely woman in with Roisin, what's her name?

FIONA. Helen.

AOIFE. Couldn't she come here a few times a week?

FIONA. She does. Thursdays and Mondays.

AOIFE. Oh.

CIARAN. She washes the whole street.

>   *(Beat.)*

BRENDA. I know it's stupid but –

>   *(**FIONA** points angrily at **AOIFE** signalling "you".)*

– I can't help thinking we're all so – that other families are –

FIONA. Are what?

>   *(**BRENDA** shrugs.)*

What families exactly?

AOIFE. Who?

BRENDA. We just seem to have more –

FIONA. – more what? More rows?

BRENDA. – we just seem to have more problems than everyone else.

FIONA	**AOIFE.**
I knew this was about Paul.	– and he doesn't want to do them.

FIONA. Aoife, will you Fuck off.

BRENDA. *(To **FIONA**.)* You're in your room all the time.

FIONA. Since when is it a crime to be a little bit –

AOIFE. Depressed?

FIONA. I'm an introvert.

AOIFE. Introvert? What are you, five?

FIONA. And depression isn't a stick you beat people with Aoife. It's an actual thing that affects millions of people.

BRENDA. You see. Now you're depressed.

FIONA. Mam, you don't have to worry about me. I'm going to help you. I'll be more useful around here I promise.

AOIFE. I'll help too Mam, I can come home more often now.

(Beat.)

BRENDA. What happened between you and Paul?

FIONA. *(To* **AOIFE**.*)* Knew it.

AOIFE. Nothing happened. We just get on too well.

CIARAN. That sounds terrible. You poor thing.

AOIFE. We're more like brother and sister.

FIONA. But you're still living together, he's in your flat.

AOIFE. Well there's two bedrooms and he pays half the rent. And it's none of your business?

(Beat. **BRENDA** *studies her tea.)*

CIARAN. Look. Everyone's miserable Brenda. Don't be fooled. Sure Roisin's in next door at ninety eight, with children in their sixties coming at her with their shit. In their sixties.

One of them has dementia, for god's sake –

BRENDA. I know, poor Larry.

CIARAN. – one of her own kids!

AOIFE. Oh, that's terrible. I didn't know that, when did that happen?

CIARAN. And the rest of them, let's face it, dreadful people. My own mother included.

(Beat.)

But it does need to be said, in fairness to you –

*(He looks askance at **FIONA** and **AOIFE**.)*

– you do have your hands full with these two.

*(**BRENDA** laughs and takes a tissue out of her sleeve.)*

FIONA. Oh here we go.

*(**BRENDA** blows her nose.)*

CIARAN. I mean who wouldn't be upset

*(To **FIONA**.)*

looking at this vision first thing in the morning –

FIONA. Excuse me, I'm gorgeous?

CIARAN. – and only devastated

*(To **AOIFE**.)*

to think they nearly had this one off their hands. And married to a nurse no less!

AOIFE. I can look after myself.

CIARAN. I can look after myself. You need a good dependable fella.

FIONA. You do.

*(They all look at **AOIFE** in agreement.)*

AOIFE. Wow. Well. You never know. Maybe I'll marry the egg man.

CIARAN. Aoife.

AOIFE. *(To* **CIARAN.***)* Once you're finished with him of course.

(**CIARAN** *jumps up from the table.*)

CIARAN. You absolute gobby bitch!

BRENDA. *(Shocked.)* No! Ciaran! What? Jim? The egg man!

CIARAN. I still don't like his eggs Brenda. I wasn't just saying that. Aoife!

AOIFE. *(***BRENDA.***)* They had a whole night of passion together.

(**CIARAN** *goes over and tries to put his hand over her mouth.*)

(Laughing.) Actually an afternoon of passion. He finishes work at lunchtime.

CIARAN. Stop talking! Everything just flies out of your mouth! Sorry Brenda!

BRENDA. Oh I'm used to it, Ciaran. In my day –

FIONA. In her day –

BRENDA. – we never told our parents a thing. Not one single thing.

CIARAN. Exactly! As it should be.

BRENDA. If we had a problem we kept it to ourselves. We kept everything to ourselves.

CIARAN. Much better days Brenda. MUCH better days. Healthier.

(**BRENDA** *sighs thinking of simpler times.*)

BRENDA. You left home at eighteen, you got a flat. You went dancing till six in the morning. You kept your coat on when you went to bed and you fed yourself and the meter. You went home any bit of leave you got and you told no one nothing

(Beat.)

BECAUSE NO ONE

wanted

to know!

> (**HELEN**, *the lovely woman, is seen travelling towards the back door.*)

CIARAN. Preach Brenda, preach!

> (**HELEN** *enters the back door in an apron and plastic gloves. She's looking shocked. After a beat everyone turns towards her.*)

HELEN. Sorry. Ciaran, pet, it's your gran.

CIARAN. What's happened?

HELEN. It's okay, your Uncle Donal's with her and the ambulance is on its way.

> (**CIARAN** *rushes out past* **HELEN**.)

BRENDA. The ambulance. Oh Jesus. Roisin.

CIARAN. Thanks Helen.

BRENDA. Fiona, look after your father for me.

CIARAN. *(Coming back to* **HELEN**.*)* Are you okay?

HELEN. Yeah, yeah, go on.

> (**BRENDA** *rushes out past* **HELEN** *and after* **CIARAN. AOIFE**, **HELEN** *and* **FIONA** *are left alone.*)

FIONA. There you go.

> *(Indicating sofa.)*

Sit down there Helen.

HELEN. I should probably go back in, should I?

FIONA. No, they'll be okay, there's enough of them.

> (**FIONA** *passes* **HELEN** *Brenda's untouched cup of tea. A few urgent "dings" are heard from upstairs.*)

He hates to miss a thing.

> (*The smoke alarm goes off, Brenda's scones forgotten in the oven.* **AOIFE** *scrunches her fists into her eyes full of sudden frustration. She runs over to the oven.*)

Go the wedding Aoife. For the love of God just go. I can't be minding you as well.

> (**FIONA** *makes her way upstairs.* **AOIFE** *takes out the burnt scones and throws the out the back door.*)

What is your problem?

AOIFE. Old people.

> (**FIONA** *exits upstairs.* **HELEN** *still stands at the back door.*)

They're always either sick or dying.

FIONA. *(Exiting upstairs.)* Jesus, Aoife!

AOIFE. Sorry, Helen.

> *(Lights down.)*

> *(Lights up. A TV theme tune plays*.* **FRANK** *moves downstage slowly with a cane. He's in*

---

* A licence to produce ONE GOOD TURN does not include a performance licence for any third-party or copyrighted recordings. Licensees should create their own.

tracksuit bottoms, plimsoles and a buttoned up pyjama shirt with a sleeveless jacket or cardigan over it. He is attached to an oxygen cylinder which **FIONA** *carries behind him.)*

*(***FRANK*** has a small bit of tissue on his face from shaving. Behind them comes ***HELEN*** carrying some wet towels. ***FIONA*** helps ***FRANK*** over to his armchair down stage right. ***HELEN*** busies herself with the towels, putting them in the washing machine in the utility room and putting on a wash. Bursts of oxygen can be heard when ***FRANK*** breathes; he's looking for something. ***FRANK*** finds his mobile on the side table beside him which he's already searched a few times and dials a number.* **FIONA** *exits into her room stage right.)*

FRANK. Hello, Frank McKenna speaking. Who did I ring?

(Beat.)

Ah my brave Elizabeth, how are you?

(Beat.)

Good. That's good.

(Beat.)

I have a little job for you, you might drop me up a couple of cigarettes –

(Beat.)

Oh, she did? Okay, goodbye.

*(***FRANK*** looks at the phone to hang up. He puts it down and starts looking for something else.)*

Hello? Hello?

HELEN. Everything okay?

FRANK. I need the gun.

HELEN. *(Confused.)* The gun?

> *(Beat.)*

I'll be with you now in one minute Frank.

> *(**FRANK** waits impatiently for a few beats and then dings a small bell beside him.)*

Yes Frank, I'm here. What is it you're looking for?

FRANK. The gun. I have the big one. It's the small one that's missing.

> *(**FRANK** picks up the blanket on his lap and looks under it. He's getting frustrated.)*

HELEN. Fiona might know where the... guns are.

FRANK. Where's Brenda?

HELEN. She's just next door, she won't be long.

> *(**FRANK** grabs at the front of his vest uncomfortably.)*

Oh, let me have a look.

> *(**HELEN** goes over and examines his chest.)*

Still a few hairs there.

> *(**HELEN** wipes the front of his neck with her sleeve and then blows on it.)*

FRANK. That's better.

HELEN. You look very handsome now.

FRANK. I wouldn't say you're a smoker Helen. Are you?

HELEN. I gave up years ago Frank. It's bad for the lungs.

*(During this **HELEN** goes looks around and takes a small mirror off the wall. She goes back to **FRANK** with it and removes the small bit of bloody tissue off his face.)*

(Holding up the mirror.)

That's better, isn't it?

FRANK. *(Smiling at himself in the mirror.)* Nothing short of gallant.

*(**HELEN** puts the mirror back and the tissue in the bin.)*

Thanks, Helen.

HELEN. You're welcome, Frank.

*(**FRANK** goes back to his phone and has it to his ear when **BRENDA** enters through the back door holding a coat and bag. On hearing her voice **FRANK** quickly puts his phone down.)*

BRENDA. These are yours Helen, I can drive you home. Where's Fiona?

HELEN. I think she's getting dressed.

*(Indicating **FRANK**.)*

We had a shave and a bit of a trim.

BRENDA. I don't believe it. What is he like?

HELEN. Resourceful.

BRENDA. Very.

HELEN. I don't mind, we had a nice time. How's Roisin's doing?

BRENDA. Donal's gone with her in the ambulance and Ciaran's following on with Aoife now in his car.

HELEN. Were they able to keep her awake?

BRENDA. She could nod her head when they arrived but it was an effort and then she lost consciousness. Poor Ciaran, she was fine this morning he said.

HELEN. She was in grand form telling me a story about her breakfast but then I noticed her breathing getting a bit shallow, so I called Donal up and he rang for the ambulance. I should probably have noticed something a bit sooner before her breath got so laboured but I was worried I was overreacting.

BRENDA. No, no, God no. She needed to go to the hospital.

HELEN. I got her hair dry at least. I'd hate to think of her down there with wet hair.

BRENDA. My God Helen, I can't believe he asked you for a shave. It's unbelievable. I hope the water was warm enough, I never put the heating on this morning.

HELEN. He doesn't like the water too hot.

BRENDA. Oh, God, was it freezing?

(Moving over to **FRANK.***)*

Well? What's this I hear about you asking Helen for a shave Frank. You know it's not her day.

FRANK. Oh. Sorry Helen.

HELEN. That's alright Frank.

FRANK. *(To* **BRENDA.***)* Havel a feel. It's a big improvement.

BRENDA. *(Touching his face.)* Very smooth.

(Beat.)

Where's Fiona? Fiona!

(To **FRANK.***)*

I'm going to the hospital to visit Roisin. She's had a bit of a turn. I won't be long.

(Beat.)

Fiona will be here, she'll look after you.

*(**FRANK** grimaces.)*

FRANK. Tell her not to plug out anything.

BRENDA. *(Amused.)* If you see her plugging anything out tell her to stop.

*(**FRANK** gestures at the oxygen tank next to him.)*

FRANK. I'm not getting much puff from this.

*(**BRENDA** moves over to look at the tank.)*

BRENDA. *(Busying herself with the cylinder.)* Let me see. It's at three.

*(**FRANK** motions "up" with his hand.)*

The doctor said –

FRANK. Fuck the doctor.

BRENDA. – to keep it as low as we can.

FRANK. Turn it up.

BRENDA. I'll put it up to four but turn it down if you don't need it, won't you? Fiona!

*(To **FRANK**.)*

And don't forget your exercises. D'you need the bathroom?

*(**FRANK** shakes his head.)*

HELEN. We went upstairs.

*(**FIONA** enters stage right from her room wearing jeans and runners and the same*

T shirt she wore to bed. She's still carrying her book.)

FIONA. I'm here, I'm here, reporting for duty. How's Roisin doing?

BRENDA. They've taken her to the hospital, she's okay, they're hoping she'll regain consciousness.

FIONA. Really?

BRENDA. Yes, really.

FIONA. I don't mean, I just mean, well, she's ninety eight. Ciaran's always saying she's fed up. I thought maybe she doesn't want to –

BRENDA. We're all fed up, what's that got to with anything?

FIONA. *(Mortified.)* Sorry Helen, that came out really wrong.

HELEN. Don't worry pet, I know what you were trying to say.

FIONA. I love Roisin, I've known her my whole life, it's not that I want her to die, I really don't want her to, I just – I thought –

*(The sound of **FRANK**'s oxygen being sucked into his nose can be heard. **FRANK** fumbles with unwrapping a sweet. While **HELEN** picks up her coat and bag from the table and **BRENDA** exits stage right and returns wearing a coat. **FRANK** pops a sweet in his mouth.)*

HELEN. Don't worry love please, we're all a bit shook by it.

*(To **FRANK**.)*

I'll see you Monday Frank. Take care.

FRANK. Bye Helen, thank you.

BRENDA. *(Clutching herself.)* I think I have everything.

FIONA. Go on Mam, we'll be fine, I'll look after him.

BRENDA. I won't be long.

> (**BRENDA** *walks over and gives* **FRANK** *a kiss on his cheek.* **HELEN** *moves over to the back door. As* **BRENDA** *approaches she exits and* **BRENDA** *follows her out.* **FIONA** *is opening presses looking for something to eat.*)

FRANK. When's your mother home?

FIONA. She only just left Dad.

FRANK. Find the gun for me, will you.

FIONA. Check under your bum, you're probably sitting on it.

FRANK. I don't think so.

FIONA. Well, it can't be far.

> (**FIONA** *gives up her search and sits down at the kitchen table to read her book.*)

FRANK. *(Annoyed.)* Where's she gone anyway?

FIONA. To visit Roisin in the hospital.

FRANK. Ah, poor Roisin.

> *(Beat.)*

Is she coming home?

FIONA. I dunno.

> *(Beat.)*

I hope so.

> (**FRANK** *gets to get up.*)

What are you doing? Wait, sit down, you'll fall.

*(**FIONA** runs over and helps him back into his seat and looks around his chair.)*

You must be sitting on it.

(Beat.)

You'll have to stand up again... hold onto my arm...

*(Hoisting **FRANK** up and back down again.)*

No, it's not there.

FRANK. That's a pity.

FIONA. *(Rooting through his things.)* It can't have gotten far.

*(She finds the gun in the small wastepaper basket beside **FRANK**.)*

Here it is... it fell into your bin...

(She points the gun (remote control) at the TV, casually at first and then with more pressure.)

Oh... and now the telly is frozen. Shocker.

FRANK. Turn it off and on again, I'm missing the football.

*(**FIONA** gets down and messes with the black box beneath the TV.)*

FIONA. It's banjaxed.

FRANK. Take out the plug.

*(**FIONA** bends down to fiddle with the TV, she makes a meal of it. On the beats she's trying different things to make it work.)*

FIONA. I'm sorry Dad but I can't handle this

(Beat.)

I don't have the patience

> *(Beat.)*

you're gonna have to wait for it to

> *(Beat.)*

unfreeze.

> *(Beat.)*

And there is absolutely no way of knowing when or how that might happen.

FRANK. *(Rattled.)* Alright Fiona, calm down.

> **(FIONA** *picks up the gun. Making one last effort she holds out her hand and presses buttons hoping for the best.)*

FIONA. With the amount of TV you watch would it not make sense to throw it out and get a new one instead of giving all your money to donkeys.

FRANK. *(Alarmed.)* What? Who's giving my money to donkeys?

FIONA. You are. Brenda had me go through all the standing orders and there were nine different subscriptions a month going out to some donkey charity.

FRANK. What else did she cancel?

FIONA. Mostly donkeys and the church.

FRANK. Oh.

FIONA. She wasn't delighted about the church but the donkeys sent her over the edge completely.

> *(A little flicker from the TV.)*

Oh thank you God.

> *(To* **FRANK.***)*

It's not frozen anymore –

(A few tries on the remote.)

but it looks like this is the only channel working so it'll have to do.

FRANK. What about the football?

FIONA. No football on this channel, sorry Dad, just midwives, detectives and life insurance ads.

(FIONA hands FRANK the gun.)

What do they have on you anyway?

FRANK. Who?

FIONA. The church.

FRANK. Not a thing.

FIONA. So what would you be giving them money for.

FRANK. Ah, stop badgering me Fiona, my head is spinning from you.

FIONA. The last thing they need is money, it only encourages them.

FRANK. Get me a tissue for my nose.

FIONA. Where are they?

FRANK. Look.

(FIONA exits stage right, the volume on the TV goes up whenever she does. The following text is heard culminating in a gunshot.)

MAN. Put the gun down.

OTHER MAN. And what?

MAN. And we can all go home. Put the gun down!

OTHER MAN. I'm going to put you down.

MAN. No!

> *(Loud gunshot followed by the Scarborough Fair ballad*. **FIONA** returns with tissues.)*

FRANK. *(Pointing at TV.)* They're always killing off that guy.

FIONA. Who?

FRANK. Him. That fella there.

> *(**FIONA** squints at the TV.)*

FIONA. The red headed copper?

> *(She takes a step closer.)*
>
> *(Puzzled.)*

Really? But he can only die once surely?

> *(Realisation dawning.)*

This must be a repeat.

FRANK. Oh.

FIONA. You've seen this same episode a few times I'd say.

> *(Mystery solved she turns to hand **FRANK** his tissues.)*

Are you crying?

FRANK. No.

FIONA. Are you sure?

> *(**FRANK** nods. **FRANK** struggles trying to open them so she opens them and hands them back.)*

---

* Licensees must use a version of the Scarborough Fair ballad in the public domain.

I'm gonna try and read one chapter of my book now. Is there anything else you need before I sit down?

FRANK. No. I have everything.

> *(Once she's out of view **FRANK** starts to dab his nose and eyes watching the TV intently. **FIONA** heads back to the kitchen table.)*

Fiona?

FIONA. Yeah.

> *(**FRANK** says nothing.)*

FRANK. Fiona!

FIONA. Yes Frank?

> *(**FRANK** waves a dirty tissue in the air, still glued to TV.)*

Dad there's a bin *beside* your chair. Especially for your tissues. Will you get a grip.

> *(**FIONA** picks up her book again.)*

FRANK. Oh.

> *(**FRANK** looks for the bin. Spots it, aims tissue, misses. He looks over and decides to say nothing and let it go but he looks down at it occasionally throughout scene.)*

What are you reading?

FIONA. You've already read it.

FRANK. What is it?

FIONA. Biography of Nico from The Velvet Underground.

FRANK. Ah. Poor Nico. She had a tough time of it.

FIONA. Right now she's having a whale of a time, but the clouds are forming alright.

(Beat.)

Are you out of books? I can get you some new ones tomorrow.

FRANK. Don't be spending your money.

FIONA. I won't be, I'll be spending yours. Just tell me what you want.

FRANK. What about Moore's Melodies?

FIONA. What about them?

FRANK. Did you get me a copy of them yet?

FIONA. No. Not yet.

FRANK. Why not?

FIONA. They're just a load of old Irish songs. What are you going to do with them?

*(**FRANK** shakes his head at her stupidity.)*

You're not gonna sing them are you?

*(**FRANK** indicates impatiently that she's interrupting his TV viewing with her nonsense.)*

They're probably out of print.

(Pause.)

Dad?

FRANK. Hmmmm.

FIONA. I'm going to ask you a question now.

(No response.)

Just giving you the heads up here so brace yourself.

(No response.)

Dad!

FRANK. What is it Fiona?

FIONA. Did you like your job?

FRANK. My job? No.

FIONA. What d'you think you would have done instead? If you had a choice.

>*(No answer.)*

There must be something?

>*(**FRANK** tries to think of a job that he'd like to do.)*

FRANK. I can't think of anything.

FIONA. Me either.

>*(**FRANK** mutes the TV.)*

FRANK. Come here to me.

FIONA. I'm alright.

FRANK. Come here.

>*(**FIONA** gets up slowly and walks over to the sofa and sits down.)*

What happened? Your mother said you quit.

FIONA. I gave them plenty of notice Dad. I had to get out of there.

FRANK. You didn't like it.

>*(**FIONA** shakes her head.)*

And you don't know what to do?

FIONA. No.

>*(Beat.)*

I think...

this sounds stupid but... I think what I'm supposed to be doing is really obvious and right in front of me and if I could sort my head out I could see it but I just, I can't see it.

(Beat.)

I don't think I've any imagination.

(Pause.)

FRANK. You're very hard on yourself Fiona.

(**FIONA** *is bit upset in a Fiona way.* **FRANK** *waits.*)

What do you like doing?

FIONA. Nothing.

(Beat.)

Reading. Relaxing.

(Beat.)

I'll be fine. I'll find something.

(Pause.)

FRANK. I think I'd have liked to go to university.

FIONA. Hmmmm. Good idea but I don't think I can do that again.

(Beat.)

Bit indulgent.

(**FRANK** *and* **FIONA** *retreat into silence,* **FRANK** *picks up his phone as* **FIONA** *browses on hers.*)

FRANK. Hello. Brenda. Will you answer your phone.

> *(Sweet.)*

Okay. Thank you.

> *(Beat.)*

FRANK. Fiona?

FIONA. Yes Dad?

FRANK. What about the guide dogs?

FIONA. I didn't cancel them.

FRANK. Good.

FIONA. Is this the Moore lad you're talking about?

> *(**FIONA** plays ["**WHEN LOVE IS KIND**"] by Thomas Moore on her phone. **FRANK** listens to a few bars and nods. The song plays out as **FIONA** settles into the couch and **FRANK** listens to the song while also watching the TV.)*

> *(**CIARAN** and **AOIFE** enter from the back door. **CIARAN** is holding a bag obviously belonging to his granny. He puts a hand on **FIONA**'s shoulder.)*

Hey.

AOIFE. *(Sniffing her sleeves.)* Ew. I stink of hospital.

> *(**CIARAN** plonks down on the seat of the sofa.)*

CIARAN. *(To **FRANK**.)* Well? You're still alive I see, she hasn't killed you yet?

FRANK. *(Smiling.)* Not yet.

AOIFE. I'm starving.

FIONA. There's nothing to eat.

AOIFE. Hi Dad.

FRANK. *(Smiling.)* Ah, me 'ole pal Aoife.

>*(**AOIFE** heads upstairs.)*

>*(To **CIARAN**.)*

I need some water. Quick.

FIONA. There's water in your jug.

CIARAN. *(Looking over at the jug.)* Bone dry. My God.

>*(**CIARAN** gets up and takes the jug to fill it.)*

>*(To **FRANK**.)*

You might as well be left here with Rose West.

>*(**CIARAN** fills the jug at the sink and drops it back over to **FRANK** filling a glass for him.)*

FRANK. *(To **FIONA**.)* Make Ciaran some tea Fiona. And bring us a swiss roll.

>*(To **CIARAN**.)*

Pineapple or chocolate?

CIARAN. Pineapple. I'm not a barbarian.

FIONA. *(Writing in an imaginary notepad.)* One pineapple swiss roll. No problem, that's no problem at all, I'll just check with the chef, there might be one in the freezer.

CIARAN. Christ this is uncomfortable.

>*(Shifts uncomfortably in his chair.)*

I swear to God you lot live like guilty monks.

FRANK. *(To **CIARAN**.)* Ring Brenda there for me. It's an emergency.

FIONA. Dad, will you leave her alone.

(To **CIARAN.***)*

How's everything down at the hospital?

CIARAN. Grand. I'm going back now as soon as I can find the energy.

FIONA. Is she awake?

CIARAN. Not yet. But every relative in the land has descended so that might account for it. They'd scald you.

FIONA. You should have stayed in the hospital and let Aoife get a taxi home.

CIARAN. *(Gesturing the bag.)* I wanted to pick up a few bits. She'll kill me if she wakes up and I don't have her lipstick.

FRANK. *(To the TV.)* You know you have to watch Aoife. Very carefully.

CIARAN. Oh you do alright. Remember the time she hid behind the door there Frank and pretended she was your dead father?

(Shaking his head.)

That was mental. No one can ever believe that story when I tell them.

FIONA. *(Gestures at* **FRANK.***)* Actually Ciaran –

CIARAN. You were just out of the hospital, off your face on valium.

FIONA. *(Still gesturing at* **FRANK.***)* Would you mind –

CIARAN. It was Christmas, wasn't it? The dream. The government should post a family supply of valium through every letterbox on Christmas Eve, shouldn't they? Like they do with iodine whenever there's a nuclear disaster.

FIONA. Ciaran!

CIARAN. What?

FIONA. D'you mind staying here with Frank for a minute, I have to find his exercise sheet.

CIARAN. Go on, I'm too tired to move anyway.

FIONA. I'll be back before the kettle's boiled.

>   (**FIONA** *exits upstairs.*)

FRANK. *(To* **CIARAN.***)* What did she say?

CIARAN. She'll be back before the kettle's boiled.

FRANK. Did she put it on?

CIARAN. *(Craning his neck to check.)* No.

FRANK. That's a pity.

>   (**CIARAN** *gets up with a big sigh.* **CIARAN** *returns.*)

CIARAN. It's on.

>   *(Beat.)*

And I did some ironing while I was at it and mowed the lawn.

FRANK. Ring Brenda for me. Quick.

CIARAN. We're under strict instructions not to.

FRANK. Don't mind Fiona.

>   (**CIARAN** *dials and waits.*)

CIARAN. Voicemail. The reception's not great on the ward.

(**CIARAN** *holds the phone out to* **FRANK** *on speaker.*)

BRENNDA. *(Voicemail.)* Hello, this is Brenda. I can't answer the phone right now. Leave a message.

FRANK. *(Officiously.)* Hello? Do you ever answer your phone? I need to talk to you. Ring me immediately. It's your husband, Frank.

(Very polite/sweet.)

Okay, thanks.

(**CIARAN** *hangs up.*)

I've one last job for you.

CIARAN. I can't give you a cigarette Frank, they'd chop off me goolies.

FRANK. I need a pair of brown dress shoes.

CIARAN. What size?

FRANK. Eleven.

(Looking at his plimsoles.)

I'm sick of these things.

CIARAN. Are you going somewhere?

FRANK. They should have a nice pair in Arnotts.

(**CIARAN** *looks at* **FRANK** *curiously.*)

CIARAN. I'll have a look the next time I'm in.

(**FRANK** *offers* **CIARAN** *one of his sweets.* **CIARAN** *shakes his head no.*)

FRANK. Your granny is a wonderful woman. Very stylish.

CIARAN. She's very fond of you too Frank.

(Beat.)

All of you.

*(Beat as **FIONA** enters.)*

Even Fiona.

*(**CIARAN** gets up to leave and as he does a loud alarm goes off.)*

Christ, what's that?

FIONA. Exercises.

CIARAN. Where is it?

FIONA. Eh – good question.

*(**CIARAN** hunts for the alarm, eventually finding it in a press.)*

CIARAN. *(Turning it off.)* Oh my heart. I'm going back to the hospital for a bit of peace and quiet.

*(**CIARAN** retrieves the bag and makes for the back door.)*

See ya later Frank.

(Calling up the stairs.)

Bye Aoife, thanks!

FIONA. *(To **CIARAN**.)* Tell Brenda everything's fine here, won't you? He's doing his exercises.

*(**CIARAN** lifts a hand in salute as he disappears offstage behind the back window.)*

*(To **FRANK**.)*

'Ya right?

FRANK. Leave it now. I'm watching this.

FIONA. You've seen it. You've seen them all.

(**FIONA** *kneels down in front of* **FRANK** *and studies the exercise sheet.*)

I can do them with you. It'll be fun?

FRANK. You're in my way.

(**FIONA** *adjusts her position so he can still see the TV.*)

I'll do them later. I want to watch the end of this. Where's my tea?

FIONA. If you do them later she'll know you didn't do them and I'll get in trouble.

FRANK. We'll tell her I did them. Just leave it for today.

FIONA. Let's just do them now and get them over with. I'll make the tea once we're finished.

FRANK. I'm tired.

FIONA. I know.

(*Beat.*)

FRANK. I need last night's football results.

FIONA. I'll check in a minute. Come on Dad, I said I'd look after you and you have to do your exercises.

(*Reading the sheet and raising one hand to shoulder height.*)

Jesus you're not going to win any gold medals with these though are you?

(*To* **FRANK.**)

You ready? Are we doing this? You won't even break a sweat. It's impossible.

FRANK. Check the tank. What's it at?

(**FIONA** *stands up again to check the tank.*)

FIONA. Four.

FRANK. Push it up to five.

FIONA. Brenda said to keep it at four max.

FRANK. Don't mind Brenda, they're my lungs.

FIONA. Okay, I'll turn it up to five, but you have to do your exercises then? Deal?

FRANK. A walk Fiona.

FIONA. One set of exercises and a walk?

FRANK. No. One very short walk. Deal?

FIONA. Come on then.

>   (**FIONA** *helps* **FRANK** *up. She reaches for her phone and puts on some house music for motivation.* **FRANK** *heads off on his walk,* **FIONA** *following him with the cylinder untangling the tube tied to* **FRANK** *as she goes. They exit stage right. Once they disappear* **AOIFE** *sneaks down the stairs and robs one of* **FRANK**'s *medical milkshakes. Once she's back upstairs* **FRANK** *emerges stage right on his own, the tube stretches behind him backstage where* **FIONA** *is holding the tank.)*

FRANK. Stop a minute.

FIONA. *(Offstage.)* We're nearly there.

FRANK. I need to get my puff.

>   (*The sound of the oxygen can be heard as he takes a few deep breaths. He's knackered. After a moment or two he starts walking again and* **FIONA** *emerges behind him.)*

>   (**FRANK** *gestures impatiently with his cane at the tissue on the floor in front of him.)*

FIONA. I'll pick it up when we get there.

> (**FIONA** *waits patiently as* **FRANK** *takes a few more puffs.*)

Are we right?

FRANK. *(Cranky.)* The football results. I want the football results now Fiona.

FIONA. Alright. Keep your pyjamas on.

> (**FIONA** *moves towards the kitchen table stopping suddenly.*)

Are you staying there?

> (**FRANK** *nods.*)

Don't move. Promise?

> (**FRANK** *nods.* **FIONA** *goes to the kitchen table and picks up her phone.*)
>
> *(Scrolling for football.)*

What am I looking for?

FRANK. Chelsea.

FIONA. Chelsea, Chelsea, Chelsea...

> *(Sounding surprised.)*

Chelsea lost.

FRANK. By how much?

FIONA. Two goals to one.

FRANK. Great.

> (**FRANK** *indicates his chair with his walking stick.* **FIONA** *lifts up the cylinder and walks to him taking his arm and helping him to his chair.*)

FIONA. Dad, d'you remember when we were kids you'd go mental at us for lying on the floor watching the telly?

>   *(Silence.)*

Dad?

>   (**FRANK** *is busy re-adjusting the tube in his nose.*)

Well, anyway, you would, it drove you mad. But it turns out that lying on the floor was actually really, really good for us.

>   *(Continued silence from* **FRANK**.*)*

All I'm saying is, if, for instance, Brenda got rid of this furniture and we all sat on the floor from now on we'd all be far less stiff. In general. That's all.

>   (**FRANK** *nods to let her know he's heard her and fixes his eyes on the TV.* **FIONA** *makes* **FRANK** *his cup of tea and leaves it beside him.*)

>   *(Lights down, lights up on* **AOIFE** *in situ at the island working on a crossword.)*

>   *(The strip lighting above the island starts to flicker.* **AOIFE** *finally notices and still looking at the paper gets a sweeping brush and hits it until it stops.)*

FRANK. Hello? Hello? What's going on?

AOIFE. Just the light Dad.

FRANK. My back is sore.

AOIFE. Aw.

>   (**FRANK** *squirms in his chair trying to get comfortable.*)

FRANK. Who's that, Aoife? Fix my cushion.

AOIFE. Okay, hold on.

> (**AOIFE** *goes over still holding the paper and tries to arrange the cushion behind his back.*)

FRANK. A little bit over to the left.

> (**AOIFE** *moves it a bit.*)

More.

> (**AOIFE** *moves it a bit.*)

Down.

> (**AOIFE** *moves it a bit.*)

More up.

> (**AOIFE** *moves it a bit.*)

Stop. That'll do.

AOIFE. You sure now? Is it safe to sit down?

> (**FRANK** *nods.* **AOIFE** *sits down on the sofa.*)

FRANK. *(To* **AOIFE**.*)* Ciaran told me you swallowed all my pills, you won't do anything like that again, will you?

AOIFE. No Dad, they're all yours.

> *(Beat.)*

I have felt a bit dizzy since I took them. Tired.

> (**AOIFE** *holds her arm out in front of her.*)

My arm feels different.

FRANK. Different?

AOIFE. Sore.

FRANK. Sore?

AOIFE. Well, not sore exactly. More like an awareness?

(Beat.)

I probably should have gone to the doctor.

FRANK. I don't think they don't pay much attention to awarenesses.

AOIFE. No. Probably not.

(Beat.)

What's this... "Remove soil-in tons initially-hand and foot."

FRANK. How many letters?

AOIFE. Five.

FRANK. Digit.

AOIFE. Digit?

FRANK. Dig. It.

*(**AOIFE** puts down her paper thoughtfully. The sounds of what suspiciously sounds like a hospital procedural show comes on.)*

AOIFE. There were a lot of sick people in the hospital.

(Beat.)

The poor man in the bed beside Roisin, I didn't like leaving him there on his own, he looked super dead.

*(**FRANK** points at the TV to indicate he's trying to listen to it.)*

He definitely needs a good turn.

FRANK. *(Suspicious.)* A good turn? What's that?

AOIFE. It's what they do in the hospital when you're on your last legs and there's no quality of life left and you can't breathe or do anything for yourself and you'd be better off dead than just lying there, d'you know?

> (**FRANK** *does not know and returns his focus to the TV.*)

So what they do is they change the bed sheets so the patient has to be lifted in and out of the bed and all the activity gives them a little nudge, gets things moving in the right direction.

> (*Beat.*)

Paul told me about it.

FRANK. (*Alarmed.*) Paul? What did you call it?

AOIFE. A good turn.

FRANK. Does Paul do this?

AOIFE. Yeah, they all do. It's humanitarian.

FRANK. (*Looking around alarmed.*) Where is Paul?

AOIFE. We broke up.

FRANK. Good.

> (*Beat.*)

Get me one of my drinks.

AOIFE. Fiona!

> (**FIONA** *enters from her room.*)

FIONA. What?

FRANK. Get me one of my drinks, will you?

> (*Beat.*)

Please.

(**FIONA** *retrieves the medical milkshake, unscrews the cap, unwraps the straw and hands it to* **FRANK**.)

FIONA. I know it seems like I'm neglecting you here, but, every bit of food in this house is frozen. Why do old people freeze everything?

FRANK. I don't know.

FIONA. I thought Brenda would be home by now.

AOIFE. Oh no. The TV is frozen.

FRANK. Will someone turn it off and on again.

FIONA. There's literally no point.

AOIFE. I'm going to bed.

FIONA. It's eight o'clock.

AOIFE. So what, I'm exhausted.

FIONA. But what are we going to do for the dinner?

AOIFE. *(Getting up.)* There's bread in the freezer.

FIONA. *(To* **FRANK**.*)* Will you eat some chips if I get them?

(**AOIFE** *heads upstairs.*)

FRANK. A few.

FIONA. *(To* **AOIFE**.*)* Can you not just wait down here until I get back.

AOIFE. I'm not emigrating Fiona, I'm only going upstairs.

FIONA. Ah come on, I'll only be five minutes.

AOIFE. Exactly. He's fine.

FIONA. I've been here all day Aoife, I'm asking you to just stay here for ten minutes, that's all.

AOIFE. And I am staying here but I'll be upstairs. He has the bell Fiona. I'll hear him.

FIONA. Fine. Off you go. You do you Aoife, you do you.

AOIFE. I will.

FIONA. Do.

> *(To* **FRANK.***)*

Just ring the bell if you need anything, Aoife's upstairs, I won't be long. Promise.

> *(***FIONA** *turns to leave.* **FRANK** *rings the bell.)*

Yes, Dad.

FRANK. Fix the TV for me.

FIONA. Ugh. I'm not much use to you there Frank –

> *(***FIONA** *goes over but it flicks on just as she reaches out to it.)*

Ah.

> *(To the TV.)*

Thank you.

> *(Pats* **FRANK***'s shoulders as she leaves.)*

I won't be long.

> *(***FIONA** *exits by the back door. It's dark now.* **FRANK** *changes a few channels, the ads are on.)*

VOICE OVER. Leopold works all day every day carrying bricks in the blistering heat. He lives in constant pain and desperately needs your help. For as little as fifteen euro a month you can help Leopold and donkeys just like him retire to one of our luxury donkey sanctuaries to live out the rest of their days in peace and comfort.

(**FRANK** *looks for his tissues, takes one out and blows his nose.* **CIARAN** *enters via the back door.*)

CIARAN. Where is everyone?

FRANK. Out.

(*Beat.*)

Aoife's gone to bed.

CIARAN. I have a present for you.

(**CIARAN** *looks around him to make sure the coast is clear.*)

FRANK. (*Perking up.*) Oh?

CIARAN. Don't get too excited, it's not brown shoes.

FRANK. (*Disappointed.*) Oh.

CIARAN. I promised Brenda I wouldn't give you a cigarette. But I didn't say anything about weed.

(**FRANK** *sits up straighter as* **CIARAN** *passes him a vape.*)

FRANK. Marijuana?

CIARAN. Yeah. Marijuana.

FRANK. (*Shaking it by his ear.*) What's in it?

CIARAN. Oil. Give it a go.

FRANK. (*Wrinkling his nose.*) Will it make my head funny?

CIARAN. Nah. It's very low quality. I wouldn't waste the good stuff on ya.

FRANK. What do I do?

CIARAN. Press the button.

FRANK. Oh.

(**FRANK** *presses the button, inhales and exhales.*)

Aaaaah.

CIARAN. What d'ya think?

(**FRANK** *takes another drag and exhales slowly.*)

FRANK. Not bad. Fruity.

(Gesturing at the cylinder.)

Crank that up for me.

CIARAN. To what?

FRANK. Seven.

(**CIARAN** *gets up and fiddles with the cylinder.*)

That's better.

(**FRANK** *takes a few audible puffs of oxygen. They're a bit stoned.*)

Did you hear about Ben?

CIARAN. Ben? Ben who?

FRANK. Ben. He's taking a woman to Arizona.

CIARAN. What woman?

FRANK. *(Over what woman.)* So she can dry out.

(Beat.)

This poor woman has a terrible drink problem.

CIARAN. Okay?

FRANK. And Ben must be –

(**FRANK** *does some calculations.*)

– seventy two? Seventy three, Seventy two? He's no great shakes himself.

CIARAN. And who is this woman? Who's Ben?

FRANK. I think he said she's from Kansas City. He has to go there first to pick her up.

CIARAN. *(Laughing.)* I'm totally lost.

(Beat.)

Is Ben a social worker?

FRANK. What? Don't be ridiculous.

(Fit of laughing.)

A social worker.

(Beat.)

Ben's a rancher.

(Beat.)

Give me another puff of this thing.

CIARAN. I don't think so!

(Car lights sweep the room.)

FRANK. Quick!

*(**CIARAN** hands it to **FRANK** who coughs and puts it back quickly. **BRENDA** and **FIONA** enter through the back door.)*

BRENDA. Hello? The house is in darkness. Where's Aoife? Frank, we're back.

(Looking around her.)

All the blinds wide open.

(**BRENDA** *busies herself closing blinds and adjusting the lighting.*)

CIARAN. Hi Brenda.

BRENDA. Oh there you are Ciaran, good. We both picked up chips so there's enough for an army. Fiona put those chips on some plates and make sure there's a plate for Ciaran.

CIARAN. I can't eat anything.

BRENDA. I know love but try and have a chip.

(*Pause.*)

FIONA. Ciaran, I'm really sorry.

(*Beat.*)

The street won't be the same without her.

(**CIARAN** *nods, he's looking at his hands.*)

BRENDA. Your family are in next door love, I gave a few of them a lift back from the hospital. They're wondering where you got to.

CIARAN. Thanks Brenda, I'll go into them now, I just needed a minute.

(**BRENDA** *and* **FIONA** *look at each other concerned.*)

They're doing my fucking head in.

(**CIARAN** *is upset.* **BRENDA** *comes over and sits on the arm of his chair and puts her arm around him.*)

BRENDA. (*To* **FRANK**.) Roisin.

FRANK. May the Lord have mercy on her soul.

(**BRENDA** *sniffs the air.*)

CIARAN. I suppose they're all in there wailing and screaming like a bunch of creeps.

BRENDA. Well… they're upset certainly.

CIARAN. Mortifying. That carry on at the hospital. Mortifying. She'd have murdered them if she wasn't in a coma.

> (**CIARAN** *sniff laughs.*)

She was a fantastic old bitch.

BRENDA. She was love, she was.

> (*Beat.*)

What's that I smell?

> (*Beat.*)

Do you smell that Frank, what is it?

> (**BRENDA** *sniffs again.*)

FRANK. (*Pointing at his nose canula.*) I can't smell anything with this thing in my nose.

> (**FIONA** *drops down plates of chips.* **CIARAN** *extricates himself from* **BRENDA** *and wipes his eyes with the back of his sleeve.* **FRANK** *hands him a tissue. They all eat a chip.*)

CIARAN. Who's Ben?

BRENDA. What?

CIARAN. Frank was telling me a story about someone called Ben?

BRENDA. Was he taking a woman to Arizona?

CIARAN. Yeah.

BRENDA. It's from an episode of Bonanza.

FRANK. Oh, yeah.

(**FRANK**, **CIARAN** *and* **BRENDA** *laugh.*)

CIARAN. The cowboy show?

FIONA. I told ye he's obsessed with it.

BRENDA. *(Laughing.)* The first time he told me that story I thought he meant his brother Ben. That took hours to sort out.

FIONA. *(To* **CIARAN.***)* What shows did Roisin watch?

CIARAN. Golf.

FRANK. When we first moved here –

BRENDA. *(To* **FRANK.***)* That's right.

FRANK. – we didn't have a car so she would give us lifts to the train station –

BRENDA. D'you remember that car? It was a great day when they put her off the road.

FRANK. – and somehow she always had the radio tuned into Golf.

BRENDA. Very boring.

(**AOIFE** *appears at the top of the stairs in a big white nightie.*)

FIONA. I always remember her ashtrays, they were little houses so when she put the cigarette down the smoke would come out the chimney. Me and Aoife thought this was the height of magic and sophistication.

CIARAN. It was.

(**AOIFE** *sits down on one of the steps.*)

I'm glad she had her hair washed.

BRENDA. Helen does a lovely job.

(Beat.)

FRANK. Did anyone change her sheets?

BRENDA. What love? What sheets?

AOIFE. Sorry about Roisin, Ciaran.

BRENDA. Jesus Aoife, you gave me a fright.

CIARAN. Thanks Aoife. Did you hear about the wedding?

AOIFE. No, did one of them not turn up?

CIARAN. Ha, look at you all excited. No, but it wrapped up at seven p.m.

FIONA. What d'you mean, everyone went home after the meal?

CIARAN. Yeah. Isn't that mental?

BRENDA. *(To **AOIFE**.)* Aoife, where did you get that nightie, is that my nightie?

AOIFE. It was in the hot press.

> *(**BRENDA** shakes her head. **AOIFE** holds up her arms to show off the sleeves which are very roomy.)*

I feel like a ghost.

> *(**CIARAN** gets up from his seat and walks over to **AOIFE** and hands her his plate of chips over the bannisters.)*

How are you feeling?

> *(Beat.)*

Devo?

CIARAN. Devo.

> *(**AOIFE** eats a chip. **CIARAN** looks at the back door reluctant to leave.)*

BRENDA. Fiona you go in with Ciaran. *(To* **CIARAN***)* Say hello love, have a drink and I'll be in in ten minutes to drive you home love.

FIONA. *(To* **CIARAN***)* Yeah, come on.

> (**FIONA** *playfully starts pushing* **CIARAN** *out the door. He stops and starts playing along and they stop and start their way out the door.)*

CIARAN. Night, Frank.

BRENDA. Aoife go up there and make sure your father's bed is pumped up. Don't plug anything out just make sure there's enough air in his mattress.

AOIFE. Aw. Why do I have to do everything!

BRENDA. Go on.

> (**AOIFE** *exits up the stairs.*)

Oh. What a day. You know they admitted his Uncle Donal as well.

FRANK. Donal? Why?

BRENDA. He fainted. Some kind of hysterical fit. The shock I suppose.

FRANK. The shock? She was ninety eight!

(Beat.)

They're a very dramatic family.

BRENDA. No one can find Ciaran's mother so she doesn't know yet. I'd say she's in Spain. She loves Spain.

FRANK. What d'you mean they can't find her, can Ciaran not just ring her?

BRENDA. She only uses something called burner phones? Whatever they are it means he doesn't know her number, she changes it all the time.

FRANK. Some people never answer their phone.

BRENDA. Why, were you ringing me?

(**BRENDA** *takes out her phone.*)

Fourteen new voicemails! Ah Frank. Did Fiona not look after you?

FRANK. In a fashion.

BRENDA. Did you talk to Fiona?

FRANK. She'll be alright. We just have to be patient.

BRENDA. You mean I have to be patient.

FRANK. We both do.

BRENDA. I'm worried about her.

FRANK. I know love. But let her alone for now, won't you?

(Beat.)

BRENDA. Oh, I forgot to tell you. Guess what Roisin's last word was?

FRANK. What?

BRENDA. Paul.

FRANK. Paul!

BRENDA. Paul.

(Beat.)

Roisin said prayers for all the people she knew every night. So we reckon Paul was probably the last new person she ever met. She loved Paul.

FRANK. I hope to God my last word isn't Paul.

> (**BRENDA**'s phone buzzes.)

BRENDA. He wants out. I won't be long love, will you be alright?

> (**FRANK** nods.)

See you in a few minutes.

> (**BRENDA** gives **FRANK** a kiss and exits through the back door. **FRANK** watches the TV for a moment or two licking the salt off his plate with his finger. The strip light above the island flickers for a bit as **AOIFE** makes her way down the stairs.)

FRANK. Hello?

AOIFE. Hello?

> (The light stops flickering.)

FRANK. Hello? Who's there?

> (**FRANK** lifts the remote/gun and pauses the TV.)

Hello?

AOIFE. Hello?

FRANK. Who's that? Who's there?

AOIFE. Tell me your name?

FRANK. My name is Frank McKenna.

> (**FRANK** reaches for a glass of water and takes a sip. He looks around a bit puzzled. **FRANK** puts the water down.)

Show yourself!

AOIFE. Is there anything you'd like to say Frank?

FRANK. I'm okay. Where's Brenda?

(Eerie silence.)

AOIFE. Is there anything, *anything* at all you'd like to get off your chest.

*(**FRANK** looks down at the front of his pyjama top.)*

FRANK. Well, now you mention it there is a chip and a bit of red sauce.

*(**FRANK** picks up the chip and eats it.)*

AOIFE. Ah Dad, you're no craic.

*(**FRANK** grabs his cane.)*

FRANK. Come on. Help me up now. Bed.

(Lights down.)

The End

ABOUT THE AUTHOR

Una McKevitt is a writer and director of original work for theatre and an Associate Artist at Project Arts Centre, Dublin since 2009. Previous work includes *Victor & Gord* (2009), *Singlehood* (2012) and *Alien Documentary* which premiered at The Dublin Theatre Festival 2016 and was the 2017 recipient of The Stewart Parker New Writing Award. *Alien Documentary* toured to Leeuwarden in May 2018 as part of the European Capital of Culture Festival with support from Culture Ireland. Her original work for Theatre has played at large commercial venues including Vicar Street and The Olympia Theatre.

With comedian and actor PJ Gallagher Una has co-written *Separated at Birth* (2015) and *Madhouse* (2018). Based on the circumstances of PJ's unusual upbringing in Marino, *Madhouse* was a critical and commercial success when it premiered during Dublin Fringe Festival at The Abbey Theatre on The Peacock Stage. In 2019 *Madhouse* completed an extensive and sold out National Tour directed by Una McKevitt and was set to transfer to Dublin's Gaiety Theatre before the Coronavirus Pandemic shut down the sector. Una has worked as a director with renowned European theatre makers Rimini Protokoll as well as with comedians Maeve Higgins (Moving City 2013) and Joanne McNally (Bite Me 2016).

In June 2021 her play *One Good Turn* premiered on The Abbey stage, Dublin to a live-streamed audience.

Lightning Source UK Ltd.
Milton Keynes UK
UKHW020702080821
388476UK00008B/251